BE

DO

Be+Do=Have

HAVE

KEVIN DU TOIT

BE • DO • HAVE
by Kevin du Toit

Published by
Doce Blant Publishing, North Port, Florida 34291
www.doceblantpublishing.com

Cover by Fiona Jayde Media
Interior Design by The Deliberate Page

PAPERBACK ISBN: 978-1-955413-15-2
HARDBOUND ISBN: 978-1-955413-16-9
ePUB ISBN: 978-1-955413-17-6

Library of Congress Control Number: 2022950583

Printed in the United States of America

www.doceblant.com

Dedicated to you, to your hopes, dreams, and desires!

Contents

Introduction

BE (Purpose) + DO (Action) = HAVE (Reward)

HUMANITY'S AFFINITY FOR LIFE IS categorized into two opposing paths: the path of good and the path of bad. Secrets to happiness will dictate how the story ends. The stories you keep telling yourself should be the stories you're living. My goal is that you are left with many happy endings. Say with emotion, feel it! BE + DO = HAVE includes time-honored affirmations, discovery, intellectual manifestations, directions about self-mastering, and the opportunity to discover life's secrets.

BE is deep faith that you have a purpose in life. DO is a multitude of calculated repetitive actions. HAVE is the expected rewards you will collect. In order to live harmoniously in this disorderly world, you will need to know your purpose, and doing so will take the right mindset.

Purpose is an encounter with your inner *be*ing. Obedience to your true purpose in life, the call of love, and trust in God gives us the faith that He is with us. Those without experience or understanding tend to hate knowledge, and yet there are those that apply knowledge brilliantly, and that leads to obedience. All around us, people live life with no purpose. We live in distress because we neglect to use the ocean of knowledge contained within our minds.

I was in a great mood because I was celebrating as I had just finished my first book. It was my birthday, the 11th of December 2018. I had spent five weeks writing my book. That act proved to me that I could have anything in this world, if I truly wanted it badly enough. The same is true for you.

Soon afterward, my book went into the hands of my writing partner, the editor, and the publishers. I felt this inner calling to write my story, a biography of my life's journey. Call it the hero's journey, of sorts. I had to get it out of me so that I could focus on writing the book. I really wanted to write.

Yes, you guessed it right, I desired to write...the one that you are holding in your hands right now. For a long time, now, I had meant to write about what had guided me, what I knew had helped many find their happiness, success in their business, love, even their calling. Little did I know that would all change. Being an employee, an epic salesman, a manager, and then CEO (becoming a master recruiter – akin to a glorified interviewer always looking for those excellent employees to add to the enterprise) gave life experience that I hold precious to this day. I was coached by the best in the industry. All I had to do was duplicate what my coaches had taught me with my clients, the very professionals I was recruiting.

I have hired hundreds of independent contractors in my leadership role, coached and mentored each to help set his or her goals, and business plans. The mentorship involved working with individuals to aid in understanding the craft in the context of their character. All of this in order to hit his or her peak performance in execution and sales. I also have over six hundred hours of training, completed within a very short eight months. That meant I spent most of my eight-hour days teaching others techniques and strategies in business development.

I credit my God, who gets all the glory, as well as my coaches, mentors, and mega agents who also deserve my deepest gratitude. Because of the massive accountability I took in replicating the trade secrets and techniques that were revealed to me, I rose to the top exponentially. The entrepreneurs I dealt with in one-on-one mentoring sessions and in training environments were taught to perform with excellence.

Show me your coach and/or mentor, and I will show you your bright future.

I also surrounded myself with exemplary people because I knew my success would come from my sphere of influence. I believe we've been born for excellence, though we act as average.

Being in leadership allows one to stand on giants' shoulders. I knew I would meet some very impressive individuals who are making massive contributions to society. Being in the shadow of business world champions had a massive effect on my ego. Therefore, I knew their success would rub off on me. I realized very quickly that when one knows where one's going, one become obsessively unstoppable. The school of hard knocks makes each of us a stronger person, and the strength I garnered created better opportunities for me. I really didn't understand until after the fact that this would be helpful. It allowed me to have a better understanding of people's behavioral traits, and how they would conduct or interact with others through one simple question:

What is your big why?

Preface

ON A WET AND EXTREMELY windy Christmas morning, December 25, 2018, I received a call from someone I love dearly. I had just seen him the day before and had heard about all the good news of how his business had grown by moving into a warehouse. At that time, he had begun to see a therapist. His seeing a therapist was something I endorsed because doing so had helped to save my unsupervised youth, my marriage, issues with abandonment and rejection, as well as bad habits I had acquired over the years. In therapy, I was shown a much better understanding of myself from countless hours of self-help guidance.

However, therapy was only a temporary solution to a permanent problem.

I quickly learned I had to focus constantly on improving my mindset and myself in general. A few sessions with a therapist set the stage for change. I learned that when the ball is in your court, do something about it! Life doesn't just happen; it happens when one wins the battle in one's mind. It's something that must take place *before* one can win the battle "out there." How you leave an impact on the world does matter, and the best gift you can give to anyone is to become the greatest *you*!

My friend and I had grown up with divorced parents, in a post-apartheid South Africa. We grew up in boarding school, "kid prison," as I would call it. There we learned through the school of hard knocks on the streets of Africa. As a child, it was a complicated, unpleasant encounter with countless disturbing events. To be utterly transparent: we had a turbulent upbringing, one of abuse, loneliness, and complete uncertainty. Our parents' decisions became the basis of a significant impact that molded the choices and values that became our characters, respectively. In all actuality, I didn't want to be a diamond like everyone else and then be cut. I had enough cuts of my own.

But I digress. Back to the phone call with my friend…

We wished each other a Merry Christmas and asked how each of our kids were doing, which was small talk, in truth. Because I rarely get calls from him, and the fact that we live two very separate lives (he's an organic junky and I am a compulsive workaholic), I knew there was more to that phone call than a "Merry Christmas," in spite of the date.

This friend of mine walked barefoot wherever he could. I always wore a suit. Our common thread in those days was to talk a few times via phone for some business coaching. He had just opened a warehouse to get more production out of his business. This friend was a prime example of his business not being a product, or a "people" business, but rather, a character-driven business. This is because *he* was the driving force behind the brand.

The call was casual for a few moments before it took a wild turn. I've been around enough crises to know that when it happens, it's often too late to prepare. Nothing comes before a thought can be processed in that situation, and only experience can prepare one to bring on positive outcomes.

I wasn't prepared for the call. His voice choked and I heard him fight emotion as he asked me, "Why am I struggling with so much baggage from my past? Why am I still dealing with past experience?" He sniffed and I could hear the pain in his words. "I'm exhausted by life's trials and tribulations, and my half-empty purpose in life." He was right. Nothing was normal about his upbringing. It was very treacherous and unpleasant, to say the least. My friend was angry with himself for many reasons: things he had done to other people, words he spoke, and the injury that doing both may have caused to everyone.

A few moments passed, and my friend began to weep. Even my headphones helped little to clearly hear and understand what he was trying to say. Almost instantly, I realized that this call was a cleansing process. I had an idea of what to do, mainly from my experience dealing with hundreds of professionals and the process they go through when eliminating their limiting beliefs, overcoming obstacles, and habits of procrastination. This time, it was different because it was personal—this was someone close to me.

He mentioned to me that he was trying to cope with past issues brought to light by his therapist, and that being in boarding school at a very young age was a big part of his current emotional state. I could relate, and remember my first night in boarding school—it was the most impactful and devastating moment in my young life—starting school at a formidable age, in the middle of a school year, and trying just to fit in. Everyone had their little clicks, or group of friends, and there was a lot of catching up to do.

Nevertheless, being left all alone on a cold concrete floor with brick walls and a sheet metal roof, I learned my place and learned to call it home.

That first night, I got into a fight with some of the kids—not a good way to start out. He had it just as rough. He told me about an older kid that came up to his bed, smacking it over and over again, just because my friend was crying. The bully told him to keep quiet because they "…wouldn't have any of that going on in the dormitory."

Brothers were often split apart as children—same with friends. It was something we didn't know how to comprehend. My friend was completely distraught from the abuse and had been carrying that issue with him for decades. I empathized with him because I had done the same—carrying anger and guilt brought on by abuse, loss, and failure in life, and in my many businesses. I spent a lot of time explaining to my friend the futility of constantly judging the future from past failures.

I have seen this behavior dozens of times when dealing with people in my position as manager and CEO of a business. Now, I was going through the same process except this time, it was different because he was my close friend, a "brother from a different mother," so to speak. His was the same story with the same subplots. I felt his pain. I knew I would because "…the closer anyone gets to the target, the more he gets shot at." I knew him as quite an extraordinary human being, and like many under the pressure of dealing with emotions, he buried his feelings for many years and chose, instead, to hide—a process that sabotages self in order to make sense of the pain that one is feeling. Human nature looks to fill in the gaps or make sense out of bad situations, even if the conclusion is incorrect.

I have found that many people sabotage their own success, instead of setting themselves up for success. Most of the time it is quite simple to see why they miss their mark—because they've allowed their emotions to be controlled by what other people have said. If you let what people say to you affect you, then you're giving them authority over you.

Let me say that again: *If you let what people say to you affect you, then you're giving them authority over you.*

This is such an important concept to take in. When we make emotional decisions, we're mostly jumping to conclusions. It's when we make logical decisions that we begin to get clarity. I have learned to lead with my heart (the sympathy side of myself) and make decisions with my brain (the logical part of me).

My friend's heart was broken, and it was Christmas Day. My family had gathered around, but he needed me the most. I figured this would be my gift to him. He had spent most of his life trying to do the right thing—striving to make everyone around him happy and filled with joy, yet he lacked it the most. He chased what he wanted to attract. I had to remind him who it was that led me to the movie "The Secret." Through his advice, I had watched that film several times over the course of many years and listened to countless excerpts from the concepts taught about manifestation.

I told him to start to become selfish—to be hyper-focused on what he wanted. The problem was that he was trying to please everyone around him. At the end of the day, he hadn't pleased anyone. He needed to be more centered on "self," which would allow him to become more purposeful. He needed to realize how incredibly special he was and what a miracle he was (and still is), so that he could move from total contribution outward to purposeful in self. He had tried to fix everyone around him when he was the one who needed fixing. Confused, to say the least, he was so busy chasing what he wanted that he forgot the importance of creating for himself. First, he would need to ultimately become, and *then* he could give away what he had learned—vast amounts of wisdom gleaned throughout all the chapters in his life.

So, I started at the beginning. I collected data by asking lots of questions, which was great because I knew that people love to talk about themselves. That way, I could collect evidence or proof, whatever you want to call it, to use as examples demonstrating where an individual's journey went off track. My friend thought he was having a breakdown, but I turned that around by calling his experience a *breakthrough*. Frequently, the homeless and the mentally ill have breakdowns but what he experienced was a breakthrough.

Let's talk about that.

My friend had enough of life and its struggles and wanted to know what the end had in store for him. I said there wasn't an end because our lives are like a book— there's always another chapter. Then when we die, we join the God of the Universe, our creator, and there we live forever—an infinite existence.

He was distraught because he had not been kind enough to other people and wanted to change that. I asked him about whom he felt that way and he said, "Everyone. I want to be kind to everyone around me."

"Well," I replied, "that's just crazy because what you want is impossible and will never happen. Besides, why would you want to do that? What has everyone done for you?"

The question caught him off-guard, and I knew that I had his attention.

I continued, "Does 'everyone' feed your children? Does 'everyone' pay your mortgage, clothe your family, fill your bank account with money, or put a roof over your head?"

I understood something that he hadn't yet realized: His beliefs were what I call "limited beliefs." In other words, we are all bound, in chains as it were, to the constraints of our limited understanding. As human beings, we tend to give authority to some force that doesn't exist. By nature, we believe in something that we don't even own. Better yet, that "something" doesn't own us. We've given permission to a belief system that is holding us hostage.

I explained these concepts to him and waited for his response. My wife could hear me from the kitchen, and I watched as she teared up. She had also experienced her own "Aha" moment then. I watched her gain her own understanding as it unraveled into truth, as I spoke with him. It was a full thirty minutes, at least, that my friend wept. At that point, it was difficult to understand him. Still, I knew I couldn't abandon him. I knew that he needed to understand he wasn't alone and that he was created for more than just his horrific past.

I relayed a story I'd heard on YouTube, in which a Rabbi stated that the ones who struggle the most on planet earth are the ones who reap the rewards of heaven when they pass.

I told my friend that his light was so bright that dark forces, the dark clouds, would try to steal his joy—his light—and that he needed to fight. He needed to be a warrior because he had to take extreme ownership of his life immediately and let go of the past. It seemed obvious I had struck a chord with him because he couldn't control his breath during our conversation. He was just too upset! That he didn't have the power to control his breath, the way one does in meditation or yoga, confirmed the difficulty he was having at that moment. How could he hang on or try to control his past when he didn't own it?

My advice: Let go and focus on today because you don't own tomorrow. Only *right now* matters. None of us have a crystal ball to foretell the future, nor would we want to, really. As Abraham Lincoln said, "The best way to predict the future is to build it."

Our reality is what we believe is possible.

This truth held for my friend as well. He began to chuckle in spite of his tears. He'd finally heard my message. I felt as if we were getting somewhere. Finally, he began to speak about this cataclysmic *breakthrough*—the one he was currently experiencing. It was not the break-*down* that he thought of before. He understood that he was not responsible for the past. His focus shifted to self-mastery, enabling him to change his existence, which would allow him to then change the people and his associations around them. BOOM!

It felt as if I had joined him in this all-conquering mood, and I found myself having to repeat concepts a few times just to make sure I made sense. Because I didn't want to overwhelm him, we decided to let those truths digest bit. We were getting somewhere, evidenced by his weeping that had mellowed, and his clarity of speech – at least enough for me to understand him better. It was a lot for him to take in, but something he desperately needed. Because I couldn't be in his presence, I had to convey a lot to him over the phone in a short amount of time—truly much to digest!

Our call ended with the golden question that I normally start all my mentoring and interview sessions: "What is your BIG WHY?"

Fortunately, we were able to talk for a while, which allowed us to cover some solid ground during our conversation. I could feel that he was in a much better place and heard him respond with the tell-tale "*Aha*" comments. So, I decided to push one more time and asked him the last question I ask of all my associates: "What is your WHY POWER?"

He didn't understand exactly what I meant—most don't, as this is a thought-shifting question. I asked him to close his eyes and look ahead with me to a time when he's seventy years old. We were far into the future. He was retired. Our kids were off doing their own things, married with kids, and we were discussing what we would be up to. He was starting to get the exercise.

Remember, each of us get to decide if we want to be great or help someone else achieve their greatness. This is an important choice we cannot avoid. Let me explain what I mean: It's irrelevant to say, for example, "I want to be a good dad." It's a given in most circumstances. To say, "I've never been to prison" is also s a given—most good people don't become incarcerated.

There is history each of us hold onto that creates who we are. But it's only history. Things are never permanent in life. Our experiences are always a permanent *part of who we are* as individuals, but that is all.

I said to my friend, "Think of it this way…when you see a hearse driving down the road, do you see a furniture moving truck behind it or a piggy bank filled with money?" Pause. "Nope. It's just a hearse. Because, when you die you take nothing with you! How people remember you is from your contribution, the impact you left behind that changed the world. It's your experience and history, and how *that* influences others is what matters, my friend."

We discussed other examples of people making purposeful choices, becoming legends. Mother Teresa cared for the destitute in the slums of India and raised tens of millions of dollars. Gandhi led a movement against British rule with a philosophy of acting in a nonviolent civil obedient way. His efforts lead India to independence. Steve Jobs gave us the personal computer.

The list goes on and on. None of those individuals took wealth with them, but each will be remembered because of his or her contribution to society.

Now, again…what is your Why Power? What is your contribution left to this world when you depart?

My friend got it and said he'd like to share his story with the world—his journey, the cycles, the pain, and the outcome—what it took to be the best person he could be. Remember, if he can't be the best *him*, then he can't have the best *around him*. Without the best, he cannot make a *best* difference in everyone with whom he associates. That's impactful! That was his profound moment—a crack in his universe that had revealed to him, his purpose.

With that, we ended our call.

+ + +

I can help you with everything you need to succeed. In truth, it wouldn't be fair to you if I didn't. My job is to share all that I have been taught and have shared with many of my professional associates in real estate professionals. To do that, I helped them make clear decisions, build road maps, a plan, and a strategy to reach their goals. I am going to share with you what you've probably heard many times before and possibly failed to clearly understand in concept or felt they didn't apply to you. Let's talk about this more.

The power of the mind is amazing.

PART 1 • BE

"The ones who are crazy enough
to think they can change the
world, are the ones that do."

- Anonymous

Chapter 1
Find Your Big Why

Let's look at the secret formula for becoming everything you've ever wanted to be!

LET ME TELL YOU A legendary story: Since the 1880's it seemed impossible for the human body to complete a mile run in under 4-minutes. For centuries it was unthinkable and considered the "Holy Grail" of physical achievement.

The legacy tells about thousands of runners who chased the dream of breaking the barrier. In truth, it wasn't so much of a physical challenge as it was a psychological belief that created an insurmountable mental block.

But not everyone believed that a 4-minute mile was impossible.

The breakthrough came on a cold, windy May 6th in 1954 when a full-time student and a man filled with belief in himself, broke the 4-minute barrier. Roger Bannister proved everyone wrong, and covered the distance in 3:59.4 minutes, on a rain-soaked track. He believed and his body obeyed.

You see…nothing is impossible.

As part of his exercise, he continually visualized himself achieving the milestone, which created a sense of confidence in his mind, his body, and his soul. Just over a month later Roger Bannister's record was broken. BE is your desire to discover your purpose in life, DO is the action you take to acquire the knowledge and skills to give understanding, and HAVE is the accomplishment, the accolades, and financial rewards to receive.

Be unashamed. Be very un-ashamed of who you are.

To be exactly who you were created to be, you need to know your *why*. That is what I call your "*Big Why*." When you realize what is possible for yourself, you will know your "*Big Why*." That is when your BE automatically appears. Then your DO, through action, will lead you to your goals. At that point, you achieve your abundant HAVE—an abundance avalanche of financial freedom and time.

Your *life* transforms you into the quality and excellence you deserve.

The genesis of this book's journey is intended to help you learn how to attract the method you will use to change your mindset and change what you bring into your life. This is so that you can have what you want. You really can achieve any goal that you set your heart's desire to. This is real and it's powerful!

Figuring out your *Big Why* will help you exponentially and give you massive motivation with purpose. My hope is that this information seeps into your subconscious mind. Essentially, your *Big Why* will reveal to you how to get in touch with your thought-life, that inner voice that will let you take control of your decisions.

Sounds a little woo-woo, doesn't it?

That's why so many people struggle with their *Big Why*—they simply don't believe. It's about faith. Having faith in self and your Higher Power to take that first big step into honoring yourself. Doing this will open your eyes and allow your *Big Why* to reveal itself.

Once you know your *Big Why*, you will renew your faith in who you really are and be inspired to unbelievable heights. Through repetition you will discover your core inspiration, your purpose kickstarts you to reach your goals. When you begin to figure out your *Why*, you begin getting insight to help your vision be laser focused. Your belief creates your reality. Next, is inspiration and gaining insight into the necessary steps to help your vision.

When I was just 17 years old, I hit a turning point in my life—a cataclysmic shift in my consciousness. I had just completed Fashion College, the youngest student they'd ever had. And I was looking for the next phase, the next chapter in my life.

We lived in a middle-class neighborhood in South Africa. The only person whom I felt believed in me 110% was my dad. He taught me from a young age that every time I wake up and look in the mirror, I say to myself, "You are a warrior, and you're going to win today's battle because ultimately, you're going to win the war!"

In fact, one night, he was home, a rarity. I sat down with him as he was going through mail and asked him, "Pops, what makes men wealthy?"

He stood up, walked over to press play on the stereo, and struck up a cigarette. It seemed I had asked him a very important question—one he needed to think about. "Kevin, I have a friend who's made it. He's got money. Let me ask him."

A few days later, Dad introduced me to his friend. He stood to meet me with an air of confidence I hadn't seen before, his back against the pub bar and said, "Say what you came here to say, Kevin."

Dad nodded encouragement. I cleared my throat, hoping my voice would sound older and steadier than I felt. "I'm looking for that one book that will change my life, develop character, and help me gain new confidence." It sounded ridiculous. I wished I had a five O'clock shadow and a few more inches on me.

"Impressive." He took a sip of whisky, stirred in ice, and stared at me for a few minutes. "I just want to be successful, like you…like my dad. I want prosperity and…"

"I get it, kid." He took another sip and set his glass down on the counter, eyeing me. "If you want resources, there's nothing better than the school of hard knocks. You'll never learn anything if you don't fail."

I didn't like where the conversation was going but nodded out of respect.

"There is one book that turned me around. I think it might help you…if you are serious and willing to learn."

"Yes, sir. I am." I stood a little taller and leaned in to make sure I didn't miss anything.

"*The Power of Positive Thinking* by Norman Vincent Peale. You can get a copy at the library." He winked at my dad who smiled in response.

"I think I've got this covered. Kevin's a warrior" Dad said and put his arm around my shoulders. Conversation over.

Within days the book showed up, set precariously on top of my dad's round living room table right beside his mail. The cover had gold Greek pillars on each side of the title, fixed against a green background. Impressive, indeed!

I took the book with me everywhere. Reading whenever I could. Within a few days, I was transformed. Committed to devouring and studying the words on each page, I vowed to create the genius that was inside me. My quality of life has never been the same because of that transformation. I approach almost everything using the processes I learned from *The Power of Positive Thinking* (Peale, 1990), a perspective filled with habits that I still follow to this day.

Labeled a warrior, and with a new sense of thought, life shifted. Convinced that I could do anything, and that nothing was impossible, I set out to conquer the world. And that is what led me at the "mature" age of 18 years to get on a plane holding a one-way ticket to Los Angeles, California. I had all of twenty dollars in my pocket. It was a swim or sink scenario because I couldn't return to South Africa. Dad said that Africa was too small for me anyway, and that America was where I belonged. I had a burning desire, bolstered with courage, to make it happen. I would be successful in America *because my dad believed in me*.

That tiny seed sowed by the belief my dad had in me gave me the strength to be whoever I wanted to be. It provided an endless amount of faith in myself—faith to move forward during the tough times, to keep pursuing my heart's desires. I was motivated by a strong feeling to achieve something big, to accomplish something that mattered. It was a hope for something significant to happen. This burning desire became the inspiration that led me to gratefully receive all that I have today.

As your *Why* becomes clear, it will feed your inspiration.

A vibration is a state of being,
the energy of a person, and
the thought of an ideal.

- Kevin Du Toit

Chapter 2
Understanding The Mind

THE DIFFERENCE BETWEEN THE *conscious* and the *subconscious* can be very confusing. The human mind is broken down into three states, studied as the *conscious mind*, the *subconscious mind*, and the *unconscious mind*. Behavior analysts explain that the differences are found in human functions and processes.

1. The *conscious mind* is responsible for all the thoughts, memories, feelings, and wishes at any given time.

2. The *subconscious mind* stores and retrieves data. Define all automatic reactions that you will respond precisely the way you are programmed.

3. The *unconscious mind* stores all past events and memories which are inaccessible. For instance, the first word we've learned to say, or how it felt to take our first step.

When you have practiced how to improve the connection between the conscious and subconscious mind by using meditation methods like the one used by Alan Silva (2022) or any vibrational meditation to elevate your spiritual life.

Inspiration creates awareness.

Did you realize that? Remember, your insight reveals where your focus needs to be. You need to see from where awareness and focused manifestation comes. That is the point of union for the two forces—it's where they meet. That is where the shift in your consciousness happens. Consciousness is you, it's the universe, it's God.

Consciousness is your *everything*!

It's your true God given core, as a human being. If you are not living the way you feel in your gut that you should be living, one billion percent the way you feel in your gut that you should be living, then you aren't being true to yourself. I am giving you permission to be selfish.

The goal here is to assist you with permanent changes, and you have to become a safe space of energy in order to invite prosperity in your universe. There's a gestation period that occurs as your awareness and focus merge, becoming one, creating a serious passionate concentration of energy. This merge gives birth to inspiration, an insight which in turn creates a path to you. When you find your inspiration, that will fuel your journey. I call it the "Hero's Journey." In turn, you begin to understand yourself.

When you know your *Big Why*, and your *How*, you will be led to action. Action solves everything. With action, you will begin to have a clear path, an understanding of how your motivation operates.

When you begin to understand who you are, your *Be*. The *Do* comes automatically, it just happens. You attract attention from the actions you take. I am not asking about who inspires you. Rather, I am asking you to look closer—look inside of you to find your true inspiration, your divine purpose on this earth. Being the best that you can be is a state-of-mind, a process of eliminating the "old you" and discovering the unique you that stands out from the rest of the crowd. Decide now to close that chapter of the old you, and begin a new fresh chapter with a brand, new you.

Doing what you love is part of the winning formula of self-mastery. What inspires you may be to read a book, learn a new skill, hike, play music, spend time with a loved one. Your inspiration is self-discipline birthed in thoughts, which are executed in your awareness. You will also begin to understand how to reject negative thoughts by redirecting your focus on something different, thus breaking inherited agreements with thoughts that sabotage your purpose in life, your contribution. Make the difference and *be* different, act, and change your life! There is monumental truth unveiled in your life by leaving behind the old lies to become extraordinary.

I am not your life guru—far from it—because I am still learning, too. I grow in the understanding of superior knowledge, and explore my faith, and the perfect universal code. I have discovered that this is known as the "Secret to the Spiritual Equation."

I remember watching *The Secret* (2021) one night after it was recommended to me. On the same day that I was given *The Secret* on DVD, I couldn't sleep. So sometime after midnight I got up out of bed and played it. I absolutely loved it, even watched it back-to-back. The concept made so much sense to me, and I felt a burden lift off me. It had such a positive impact that

I felt I could see my life in a clearer, more purposeful way. What *The Secret* didn't do was provide a formula, a kind of recipe to follow on how to live a more purposeful driven life.

I did research afterwards and even read the hundred-year-old book *The Science of Getting Rich* written by Wallace D. Wattles (2020). This is the book that was supposedly an inspiration behind making *The Secret*. That is how it all began. *The Secret* revealed what happens when we change our mindset, and *The Science of Getting Rich* inspired me with a kind of GPS for what I need to do, to have in life what I desire.

Ninety-nine percent of people are not willing to do what it takes to make their dreams a reality. You are the one percent. Now, if you did just one thing—work that one percent each day towards having the life you desire—imagine what would happen. Lock out the world's commentary, block out other people's opinions, and take responsibility to make a difference in your life, beginning now. Your life is your responsibility, that's the power you need to take over extreme ownership in self.

Awareness is a very important part to notice your change. It is vital to understand how awareness can change your mind. It's incredibly powerful to know how much you can raise your awareness. Tangible and real results in yourself take time. You will become what you are meant to be once you realize that you are aware. It's called growth. None of us know what we don't know, and when we become aware that we *are aware*, we begin to think clearly, see clearly, and act clearly. We all behave with *unaware* because we don't know we are in that state. Belief in our own circumstances can be misleading when we lack awareness—it is only because our mindset makes us think we're so on top of things. But remember this, no one can purchase awareness. None of us can buy that state of being aware.

Awareness comes from truly knowing yourself.

Few rarely seek knowledge or understanding, and leaders often abuse power that we give them because we, without adequately vetting many of those people, put them in power in the first place. We seem to live in oblivion with our minds unconscious of action, or lack thereof. Everything seems to happen around us when we don't do anything.

We see such abundance everywhere, yet we live in lack. Why is that?

Those who have tapped into their consciousness seem to be on top of the world. We are in search of a miracle—a miracle to give us the boost to separate us from our past or current state. The practice of human consciousness is an evolution that allows the discovery of a secret equation. A lot are calling this the Second Mind. However, I believe you are already a part of your Second Mind.

Everything is one. We are all one—an extension of The One. I am not here to inform; I am here to teach. There are no secrets if we but seek them out. They will be revealed and that's when you reach into your consciousness. You will evolve when you become focused on what you are passionate about achieving—a vision, a goal. When logic and emotion join at that point that you *want* to achieve, you have what you desire. When your mind (brain) and your emotions (heart) join forces, you create awareness of the internal mind's activity and you become conscious of the thing you are inspired by emotionally. This is the power of visualization.

This image gives a simple view of this truth:

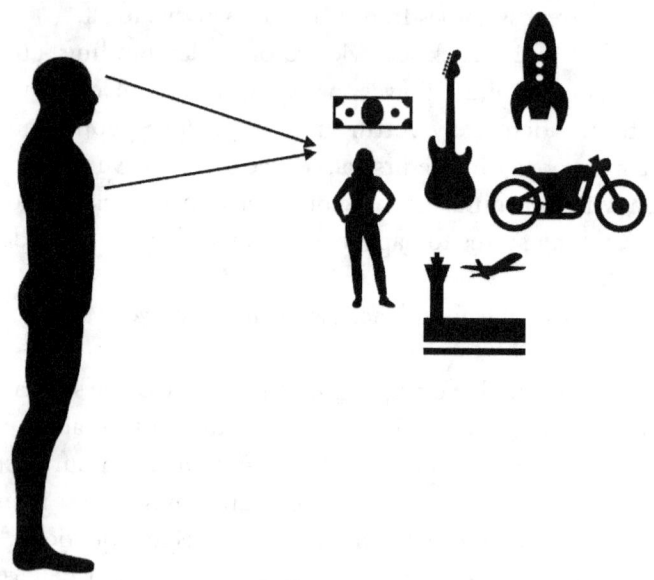

©2022 Kevin du Toit

When you know what you want in that visualized goal, dream, or object, your desire will be inspired emotionally to take action, and your consciousness will make you aware. Voila! You have what you want. The mind and heart join-forces to manifest your reality.

They who are wise
shall be humble.

- Enoch

Chapter 3

The Second Mind: Subconsciousness

BEING EXTRAORDINARY SOMETIMES JUST HAPPENS. In this book, I merely share with you my direct revelation of incidents that led to my hero's journey, and the best way to describe this adventure is by telling my story. These are the endeavors I can share with you about what I experienced. What I am hoping we can do together is create a better world, a better environment, a better understanding of who we should *be, your purpose…* and what we're going to *Do*. Action solves everything, *Have* brings the rewards, and your contribution is leaving a legacy.

Programming encompasses us in every way. Let me list a few items to help better explain the body's programming. The physics of the human body and mind. Our biology is a massive matrix embedded in tissue that allows us to walk, talk, and think. Taking care of our bodies seems hard at times. However, it's quite basic—eat healthy, walk regularly, and feed the mind. We are such complex creations that it's awesome to know that 60% of our bodies are made up of water. And it's crazy to think that an adult takes an average of more than 20,000 breaths a day. What blows my mind is that the brain contains 86 billion nerve cells. Our kidneys process approximately 50 gallons of blood and about 200 quarts of fluid on a daily basis (2022). Only once did I change my genetic coding by reprogramming my thoughts, feelings, and purpose. When I better aligned my intent with what God wanted for me, I experienced a crack in my personal universe. Everything changed, the trajectory of my circumstances improved times-ten.

Our programming stems from the moment we are conceived in our mother's womb. For instance, I experienced rejection, betrayal, and abandonment before I saw the light of day. My mother's boyfriend got her pregnant with a sperm count that was one-in-eight million chance of being viable. When he found out about her pregnancy, he left my young mother to fend for herself. My adoptive dad, a heavy drinker and still my hero, left us when I was eleven. We moved to Johannesburg, in South Africa—the biggest city and capital of the Gauteng province.

It's called the "City of Gold" and began as a 19th century gold mining settlement. My mother was working full the time to support us while the family took care of my brother and me. My life was lived carefree – more on the street than in a classroom. Sadly, that led to more trouble than should have for a child. For example, I crashed my mother's car at 14 years of age. By the age of 15, no school in the district would accept me, due to my destructive behavior. It went on from there (hundreds of pages of events that would fill an entire other book. Perhaps later, I'll write that saga).

The point is that my programming was off. It wasn't excellent and where it should be, considering that my IQ was 185. I am not tooting my own horn, and I certainly have had my fair share of failures, far more than most people I know; but the importance of recognizing when one is far from his potential is seen in my antics. In truth, my IQ level doesn't really matter anymore, it's what I am *doing with it* that counts. Let me put it this way. Mensa is the Top 2% of the population. My mother is in the 0.6 (point six) of the Top 1% so that places me 0.1 (point one) of the Top 1%.

My IQ was off the charts considering Einstein had a possible 160 IQ. It took me into my forties to realize I had missed out on almost a lifetime of opportunities because of my programming. I thought I had a positive attitude and was eventually shown that wasn't true either. I decided I'd had enough because I saw too many repeated cycles of self-sabotage, negative thinking, and internal insecurities that made no sense. I knew there had to be more to life than a moderate existence, living paycheck-paycheck, and never satisfied at work. It made no logical sense to live with zero purpose. I saw greatness all around me and the massive contribution that was left behind by people like Henry Ford, Steve Jobs, Mother Theresa, and Nelson Mandela, just to name a few.

One day while in Las Vegas, I woke up in the ER. Finally discharged after four days stay, I was diagnosed with Transient Global Amnesia (TGA). I had a mid-life crisis…I was only making about $100k a year in my mid-forties and, with the responsibility for five sons, the reality of what had happened made me think about how I needed to leave them a legacy. At the rate I was going, I would leave them an inheritance of debt instead of a gift. I was not going to let it end this way. Bedtime for me was at 9:00 p.m. and awake at 3:30 a.m.—my new schedule.

My daily routine, every single day, was hourly Bible study beginning at 4:00 a.m. and then time in prayer and meditation for an hour at 5:00 a.m. with God. On my commute to work, I listened to inspirational speeches and Christian motivational content. This, I continued with every spare moment I had. I began to watch lots, and lots, and lots, of YouTube videos on how to change my situation. With every self-help guru I listened to, I found a common theme.

Something needed to happen. I needed to flip the switch by changing my energy—to focus on abundance instead of lacking. Believe me when I say that I thought I had lived with a healthy mindset. Clearly, I wasn't.

Once I began to practice what I had learned, everything was *for* me, and nothing was *against* me. I started to receive massive promotions. I went from my original goal of making high commissions through high closed sales volumes, to making even higher commissions with unimaginable closed sales volumes.

This book is meant as encouragement. Like so many others who are seeking change, it's important to realize that it starts with altering the way we think. The mind is the powerhouse. It's very similar to building a house. If the best materials are used and every brick is placed precisely where it belongs, then an outstanding home will be constructed. If our minds are fed negative, self-deprecating content, then that controls thoughts and we generate an unstable existence. You give yourself an unfair love relationship because of how you feel about yourself.

Thoughts become things. Everything that you have accomplished in wealth, relationships, and objects had their beginning in a vision. You were the brainchild of your thoughts, which are manifestations of your energy coming into existence. Your heart desired a certain outcome and so you focused on that vision. When the desire and thought met—BOOM!—miracles happened and you brought your vision into existence. Together, we will build the temple of the mind. We literally must think of our minds as a battlefield that needs protection. Be a warrior by going out every single day with the intent to win the battle, so that at the end of the day, you can win the war. Don't allow just anything to enter your mind and captivate it because you need to stay focused on the affirmations in order to create what you desire.

You are here, right this moment, reading this book, because you are embracing a massive change, and it all started in the realm of thought. The purpose of this journey is to plant seeds of productive, positive affirmation to manifest the most magnificent *you*. I want you to look at the greatest secret equation in its complete form: "Start with the end in mind."

Do this so that you can see the end in mind and then work towards it. It may look like a modern-day puzzle—that's exactly what it is. If you know what you want to accomplish by reading this book, then your journey will be more fulfilling and give you a clear path to where you want to go. In every race you know there is a finish line, and if you get there first, you win. There's always only one winner of a race. In this race we know there is a finish line and what that looks like, so we have a more driven and purposeful outcome. What if you really wanted to have everything your heart ever desired in life without having to give up anything?

Every day starts and ends with the sunset. In just the same way, think of the end in mind, the finish line. This pertains to everything in life. A meal is never just eaten: One knows what one wants to eat, then prepares the meal, cooks it, serves it, and then eats it. One knows what time to be in the office, what the job entails, what time to go home, and when the paycheck will be received. We all know that what we put into your bodies, will affect how our bodies survive. Whatever you put into the job, you'll get the same out of it.

This formula was designed to groom for excellence. When followed, we take ourselves from being followers, to being LEADERS. It's meant to be a guide to success. No one can just wing-it every single day in life. We all know we work in some capacity for a paycheck. We work the weekend, we work to eat, we work to live, we work to pay bills, and we work to make other people happy, healthy, and wealthy.

Now is the time to do this for yourself.

It isn't necessary to be über-smart or part of some wealth-building network. This isn't how success is done, and it's not rocket-science…it's a formula that is used in everything that's accomplished, and the best part is that now you hold it in your hands. You can touch it, feel it, and own it…all in the palm of your hands.

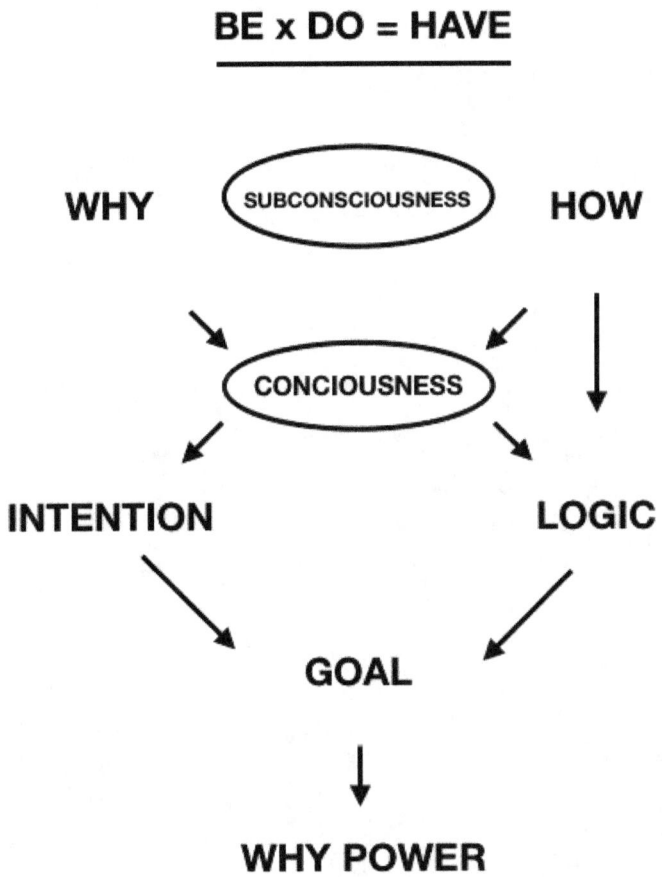

PART 2 • DO

If you only knew the
magnificence of the 3, 6
and 9, then you would have
the key to the universe.

- Nikola Tesla

Chapter 4
Visualization Opulence

WHO, WHY AND WHAT AM I doing here today?

Stop and think for a moment about this question before you continue. And while you read, ponder on these words.

Making a habit of asking this question daily, first thing in the morning, helps the daily routine be far more purposeful than in just another ordinary day. After finishing this book, drastic changes in every area of life will be evident. I want to help take your ideas and make them your story. I want greater happiness for us all, and I call it the ping-pong effect. So, let's entertain ourselves and pretend with me, for a minute, that you have a ping-pong ball which bounces very easily. It's super light, bouncy, and a blast to play with!

Now, take the same ping-pong ball and drop it into liquid nitrogen. Once the ping-pong ball lands in the nitrogen it's composition (it's "nature") completely changes—a metamorphic transformation takes place. Now, drop the ping-pong ball onto the floor. It shatters into pieces. It almost disintegrates. The ping-pong ball went from being this light bouncy object to a piece of glass. It transformed drastically.

That's what it's all about as we transition from our physical world of matter, to an almost out of body experience where there's no physicality—the divine world—a world in which we merely partake. When our lives move (from this world through the transformation from superior knowledge, which isn't powerful until we apply that knowledge and understanding we take on a new form) we discover the remarkable person within ourselves. Our true being!

Once one figures out the reason to do something, and how to do it, that person will have what it takes to be the desirable self. In truth, by reading this book and understanding its concepts then acting on the principles herein, you will embark on one of the greatest spiritual journeys you'll ever experience. And here's the science behind it: This isn't E=MC2, or some masterful Hollywood movie-type gift in mathematics, it's an equation you already possess. The *secret* before the secret is the *law of action* before the law of attraction. To BE comes first, and that is everything that you are, and or are not. Whatever you are aware of is either lack or abundance.

Here it is: BE + DO = HAVE. Also known as the *Secret Spiritual Equation.*

Here is an explanation regarding Be, Do, Have.

You may consider it a law, a practice, a principle, or even a spiritual journey that is described as a guide to success…you can have it as well. For you to utilize the law of success, all three stages have to be in effect. This creates a reality. The belief that to just crush it every day by working hard, long hours, seven days a week, and create a life with little money, bad relationships, and failing health is false. The opposite is true. Belief in your goals and dreams, with unaltered faith that you deserve every bit of those aspirations, brings abundance. Success is defined individually, so however you define success as, that also will be yours with the same kind of belief.

DO is the action part, and it must be done with purpose. You can take action all day long in whatever pursuit you choose, without a clear goal or destination in mind, and the same thing happens—your massive action breaks you and likely gets you into the grave faster than anticipated. You must have a clear vision, a goal, a plan to reach your destination successfully. This is akin to a game plan.

These are adventures discovered along life's journey. Lessons in life are the reason behind motivation. When we don't feel worthy, our state of being is filled with lack stirring us to do better. It doesn't matter what you do. Anyone living with this thought process, will always find little to no fulfillment with life's circumstances. This is incredibly important to comprehend because our super-power is our WHY-POWER.

What exactly does this mean? Why would anyone want to BE someone that is extraordinary, remarkable, or have massive purpose in life?

The answer lies in what comes next. You must have the DO. In fact, DO is how you become the BE. Your BE passion—your heart's desire—drives your inspiration, which will fuel your ingenuity. Living this way, you will know your WHY.

The process to discover the DO comes from the creative logical forces inside the mind. This is your vision about what needs to be done. Once you know your passion, your logic locates the direction (much like the GPS in your car or on your phone) to get you to your location. Once there, logic and thought helps to achieve your passion. Ask from where passion originates—it's not from thought, it's from the heart—the desires of your heart. The heart's desires come into reality when consciously aware of who we are. Consciousness is the state or quality of awareness of God—being aware of something within self.

BE is the instinctive element of self. It's the natural part of *you*. The DO part represents what you intend to *do*. You will always BE yourself, that's who you are. It's what you DO, the action you take, that changes your outcome.

DOing is the thing you do to affect your BEing.

The feelings you have, your thoughts, and purpose are all related to the DO. The moment we shift thoughts into BEing, everything changes. It sounds a little confusing but think of it this way: When asked "What do you do for a living?" the answer usually comes in the form of BE, "I am a writer" or "I am a nurse" or "I am a realtor." That concept of what is *believed* about who the one is and how someone views him or herself begins to attract an energy of abundance. This belief is a manifestation of intention, bringing in what one desires in life. It's a play on words, really. To BE in battle with negative thinking and change that thinking will ultimately change individual circumstances. When an individual begins to think about self differently, both the person and his/her circumstances will likewise change.

What you think about, you become.

I call this the Law of Success, and, of course, success means many different things to many different people. For instance, success can mean losing weight, being happy, finding love, getting a desired job, taking dream vacations in exotic locations, and so forth. The list is endless.

We have not, because we ask not.

An upgrade in expectations will bring about the forced upgrade in those expectations. My desire is for us all to experience a life we'll never forget. Remember, a change in thinking is possible because it's the only thing over which we have total control.

Some fascinating facts about the human body: The odds of being born is one in four hundred trillion or more. There's a better chance of winning the lottery! The probability of existing at all is one-of-a-kind. Humans are unique specimens, to think in science terms. There is nobody else in the world like you! Why don't people see how remarkably incredible are the opportunities for them; that nothing is against them because each of us is awesome, wonderfully made, that we're the secret?

Not many are aware that the human skeleton is completely replaced every ten years, and the tongue, just like fingerprints, has its own one-of-a-kind unique print—same with the irises in our eyes. Here's a stately fact: our bodies are made up of a mind blowing seven octillion atoms, that's twenty-seven zeros following the number seven (7,000,000 ,000,000,000,000,000,000,000). The body contains within itself nearly one hundred trillion cells (100,000,000,000). Bones, which are four times stronger than concrete, muscles, and tissue cells provide structure to form your entire body—the same one you see in the mirror every day.

There's no need to be frightened by the word bacteria because there are approximately ten times more bacteria in your body than total are cells. Our bodies are colonized by hundreds of different kinds of bacteria, most of which are considered "friendly." We breathe an average two hundred thousand times (200,000) and there's no off button—we can't just switch off breathing whenever we decide to. Not even the wealthiest, most powerful people in the world can decide when and when not to breathe.

Crush negativity! Cancel it verbally. A negative response is a choice—it's our fuel. The next time you feel negative or sad about who you are, do an online search for "amazing facts about the human body" or "history of the world" and you'll soon realize how massively significant you are to be a part of creation. To be where we are at this point in history—the best time ever—is phenomenal because more millionaires are born in one day than ever before. To be accurate, it's over one thousand seven hundred thousand (1,700) millionaires are made each day worldwide.

Know this—you can be one of them because there is nothing that can stop you. We live in the heartbeat of the world, the United States of America, this is the last best place left, and if you've got problems with America, clearly, you haven't traveled much.

"So that you will succeed in all you do and wherever you go."

- Law of Moses

Chapter 5
Speak Into Existence

THIS IS WHERE WE BEGIN to realize the value of our internal Source—something that will supply all our wants and needs. I have had multitude of consulting sessions with entrepreneurs, and I always start with this question, "So what's your "Big Why?" Almost every time, I get a blank look, as if the person sitting across from me has never heard that question before. It seemed to be a foreign concept for most.

Remember, my job is to groom professionals for excellence. I know what questions to ask and which questions to avoid. When recruiting or interviewing an individual, this question almost always opens a Pandora's Box, of sorts—the question introduces a conversation that the interviewee never saw coming. Think about it for a minute.

"What is your big Why?"

This is a soul-searching question—a command—because that's exactly what it is designed to be. In fact, there are only two questions that, when asked, will allow the other person to open up. "What is your big Why?" is the first. The next is, "What is your Why Power

Many individuals have no idea about why they do what they do. People seem to comb their minds for an intelligent answer, and most times, it leads to an exploration into self and thought because it *is* such a deep question. Knowing your *why* in life is important. It's illuminating. The purpose for why we exist is the fuel that drives our desires. The *why* is the cause for people to resolve whether they've made the right decision in life.

This is what I see. These are the people who come to me for advice and guidance. It is this type of reasoning that allows me to work with someone and watch that person blossom into his or her potential.

As humans, we change jobs, take on a new education, or relocate to a new city or state because we desire to make more money. This is a good focus! It seems as if money solves a lot of problems. With money, one can buy the "good things in life." It doesn't end there, though. We all know there is more to life than just money.

Right? Think about this for a moment.

"Money does not make one happy." That's easy to say. Look at what money does for someone: Health, happiness, and prosperity. Those conditions make one *very* happy and money plays a big part. Without money you cannot support your health or gym account. Happiness comes from freedom, and that's only possible if you have a nice cushion in savings. To have enough money to DO the things that make you happy brings prosperity. It's a personal view—prosperity. You define what that means and how it looks in your life. And there is a cost to that as well.

Deep, down inside our inner core being, to the world that resides inside our bodies, is a royal crown of energy seeking more out of life than just a job. This energy wants to make more for you than just money. I get how this works because this is what I do for a living—I help lift others. I endorse my staff and business associates; I help them to discover excellence within themselves, to show up every day with the mindset to reach peak performance.

Knowing your Big Why is the way to manifest what you want to attract, from where you were to where you are going. Don't think you own your past because you don't—it's over and doesn't exist any more than a pre-conceived notion of what the future will be. The past is over. It's an event that happened and is finished. Letting go of the past is the best gift you could ever give yourself. Choose to not allow the past to have any authority over you. The future is where the glory days are waiting, even though, those days don't exist yet.

On many occasions, the person I am interviewing or mentoring tilts his head like a little puppy. It's a natural response to the question and, *Bam*! I've got him. Now the journey starts. To discover their true meaning as to why we are in each other's presence at this exact moment in time is exciting. I remind my client that at this moment in time, he/she is the most important person to me, and he/she has my undivided attention. This gives us some time to seize the instant they rediscover who they really are.

This question is intense, especially given the fact that the client is in an interview, a process to see whether we can work together. Most times the client's prepared for getting the job, but instead, he is asked to seek that "forever young magic" they've been hiding under their personal complexities of life. I would keep quiet, and it would get uncomfortable, which was exactly the goal, as we transitioned into digging deep to find that meaningful answer to Why.

Sometimes, the process necessitates a philosophical moment with the client because a career change, more money, and a giant leap of faith in self had never really been explored in a discussion before. My approach would include radical concepts like, "I believe we've been lied to" or "Nothing is really what it seems to be." That's when the intellectual in someone comes out.

Many times, I saw people sit up in their chairs, or nearly leap out of their skin, even break out in tears. Emotion takes control most of the time because nothing can stop someone when she wants more out of life. These clients felt as if they'd finally met someone who understood. This is such common behavior that I know exactly how it will play out, and therefore, out of respect to each person, is to let him or her discover the Why in their life—the truth of existing in our universe.

It is a kind of magical experience. Time coaching individuals helps them to recognize a hero's journey. Our time together is more than just an interview. There, we take what's on the inside and bring it out, like wearing your heart on your sleeve, so to speak. The power in this question became clear the more I queried it, and the more I understood, I recognized how important it is.

This was a very special moment, a love affair of words, an experience, and an opportunity for each person to rediscover the leader inside. This was exactly the intention; to reveal their greatness, to know that there was more to life and that they deserved to know what that was for them. If a conduit to bridge the transformation happened, then so be it. I was their go-to-person now, then, and afterward. My client left knowing she didn't have just another day in life. I knew from experience our time together would be therapeutic, and I also wanted her to leave with something significant. Even if we didn't work together going forward, that would be okay. I knew she would, at least, feel better about herself and have some clarity about the journey she had just chosen to embark upon. Digging deeper into one's consciousness helps to understand who one really is. That allows me to support and to not "let down." Our interaction would be unique and wonderful because she would have revealed her own creative genius.

The revelation wasn't about money, asking the Big Why mostly led to seeking more out of life than just a paycheck. These people knew that what they were doing in their lives or career wasn't fulfilling or giving the excitement they needed to thrive. Whenever we make changes in life, it's mostly because we feel internally that something isn't right or that there's more in the world to offer or be offered.

I believe there's greatness in every one of us. It takes the circumstance to spark that glory. Then, we start to ask ourselves internal questions as to why we are here. Many times, people got very emotional, holding back tears because something spoken had obviously hit a soft spot.

This is my specialty.

Action solves everything.

- Anonymous

Chapter 6

Achieve Massive Action

WE'RE *all* SPECIAL.

So, what does that look like for you? For me, I would fall back on dad's favorite word: Magic. Whenever I get the chance, I like to drop that word, "This is a *magic* moment, don't you think? What's so wonderful about your life right now?"

When asked that question, there wasn't much magic in life. It seemed then a spark of freedom had been lit because a boss showed the compassion of a friend by asking a "magical" question. People need the magic of closeness and comradery more than fear. We have lived long enough to have created many behaviors, habits that are mostly destructive; but in serving each other we eventually become free. As humans we're habitual. While bad habits lead to bad behavior, good habits lead to good behavior.

My purpose by asking the Big Why question is to help set people free. With that, my clients could walk out of our time together feeling fulfilled instead of empty-handed. People generally mean well. Most desire purpose in life.

With histories such as dysfunctional parenting, archaic schooling, and a few bad choices, many are left broken.

My belief is that, as a people, we've been utterly lied to—by parents, by teachers, by society, by loved ones, and by that pessimistic friend who must constantly remind us about all the negative events in life. Most of us believe what we have been told, and we want more out of life, as a result. We look for certainty and want rapid, on-demand results, which is not how life works. Initially, be aggressive but then be patient and wait for the results. It's easy to count from one to twenty-one, however it takes seven thousand six hundred and sixty-five days (7665 days) to turn twenty-one in years.

Most responses about the Big Why is that the individual wants to make a positive change in the world. That is the way of healing insecurity, which I would explain, is the process of improving self *first* before sorting out the rest of the world. Change doesn't come from "out there," change comes from within. Then you can have an impact on your surroundings, the world around you. How can anyone want to make a difference in the world when s/he doesn't understand self? So, let's figure out what needs to be done first. Let's be selfish, for a moment, and figure out what is your Big Why?

If you've had children, like me—five boys(!)—you get well-versed in discipline, reprimands, love, and guidance… all in one session. My boys are warriors, and each one is traveling along a different life-path. I've acquired the understanding to support whatever they desire to do (or be) in life. I endorse their music, ideas, and gaming with expectations of them doing great things in each of their individual endeavors. I never take away. I always come from a place of contribution, and then I let them figure out what they want to do with it. It is the same with my interview sessions—I always start with the Big Why and then I share the journey with each client as we go into a world of self-discovery, which I call self-mastery.

While it is hard to experience life alone, I have enough experience in doing just that—growing up on my own—so this is nothing new to me. Let me share this illustration: When I first arrived in America, my first job was to print pictures in a One Hour Photo Lab. The customer would drop off their camera or some 35mm film, and my job was to develop the film through a chemical process then individually expose each image onto paper. It was a magical process because as I would meet the customer, I realized that most of the time that undeveloped film was a prize possession. Often, the customer would share details about the amazing family vacation they just had, a wedding they just attended, their toddlers first steps, or memories of loved ones.

Now, we live in a digital world and the process of developing film through a One-Stop shop is a thing of the past. Still, there is nothing like holding a memory in your hand—one that you can feel as it touches your heart. Tangibility is something that cannot be replaced by technology. It was special to see people's memories come to life, as I selected each image to be printed on the photo paper. What blew my mind was that if you just looked at the 35mm film in the dark room, nothing was there—just a brown piece of 35mm film. But when treated with a chemical process, the images magically came to life.

I saw this same process occur daily with everyone I interacted with in the interview process. That's the way it is to this day whenever I asked about the Big Why. It is that "aha" moment, a deliverance, an instant healing as I help to expose the answer.

Faith is strong within, and most are looking for glory. It's easy to be a follower, to work with entrepreneurs in that "follower" role. The Law of Faith tells us that whatever we want, whatever we desire, if we believe that we can have it, then we, indeed, shall have it. Fight for your faith and believe, especially when you can't see it in the physical. Know you can achieve your goals in the real world, in real time.

We receive the promises made when we demonstrate our faith in the things that are not yet a reality. Everyone I have the pleasure to meet has such amazing gifts. This truth was right in front of them. I could see it, but why couldn't they? This is the million-dollar question. Putting ego and pride aside, a lot of time would be spent discussing the Big Why. Then we'd look at the action available to them, opportunities to reach their results. Every day was an experience to blow the socks off the interview process, and if I didn't, then I would learn from it to keep perfecting my craft of being a game-changer.

Do you want to pay off your debt, buy a sports car, a dream home, a mega yacht, an exotic vacation, the honeymoon you never took, or support an orphanage? Once you know what your Big Why is, you should write it down—wet ink on dry paper, preferably in a journal—so that you can meditate on it. This is where the magic begins. When the logic, the *how* part of your goal, knows your Big Why, it will charter a course to attain it. This is the greatest secret—a perfect equation. When the heart and the mind meet, goals are attained.

There it is! When your desire and your game plan meet, at that magical point you achieve your goal, you make that dream come true. Without a *why* merging with your *how* it will be impossible to reach your *goal*. The laws of success need to meet up, like the blade of a sword, and voila: Goal accomplished.

Here's some examples of a BIG WHY:

- Faith - be a river not a reservoir.

- Family - legacy forget about me it's all about you.

- Impact - you've got to have contact.

- Optimal health

- Time = Life

- Money = quality

- Lifetime of adventure—an experience.

- Travel

- Dream home

- Dream car

Ask yourself now: "What is my Big Why?"

PART 3 • HAVE

God created human beings
with the deliberate intention
of sharing the ordering
of creation with them.

- Book of Genesis

Chapter 7
The Hero's Journey

THE WORLD IS FULL OF get-rich-quick schemes and on-demand knowledge, yet it's filled with the wealthy and the impoverished. A great lesson in life is to learn from everyone around you. There's an amazing YouTube video of Jim Carrey, who needs no introduction, and how he went from broke to stoked on a check he had written out to himself a few years before. The amount was for ten million dollars for a movie he would star in one day in the future. Daily, Mr. Carrey would visualize and remind himself of the check he kept in his wallet. This was an opportunity waiting to happen, in Carrey's mind. Well, it eventually came to pass and Jim Carrey was paid ten million dollars. This is money he knows he manifested into existence because he used his energy to achieve that goal.

With a clear objective in mind, we can accomplish great things. Success is like fine wine, it's an acquired taste. It's easy to say, "Just believe in the Law of Attraction." However, there's a key element missing in that comment—it's missing the beginning of what it is you want to attract. What does that mean? You believe you can attract money. However, that's easier said than done. You need to attract the activity, the action first, in order to create the energy or Universe, if you want to create money or any kind of abundance.

It takes a set of skills which will feed the mindset and then the work. The activity will invariably bring money into your life, and the more you practice and work hard and smart, the more you attract. It's a part of the compound effect—you have to, first, put in the effort. Whether it's blood, sweat, and tears, or brain power, before you see the rewards. You need to *become* what you desire because faking it is not real, and the return will be fake too. "Fake it till you make it" is meaningless. There's no such thing as trying.

The moment you focus your vision into action, you'll learn new patterns which will create incredible glimpses into what's possible. A good practice is to stop and look at your surroundings the next time you're out. Discover the many retail outlets, the vehicles, fashion statements, technology platforms, and broadcast media avenues. There's something they all have in common—at one point in time, none of these businesses were real. Someone dreamt up the first flight, a motor driven vehicle, cutting edge technology...all of it...like mobile phones used to crunch time and exponentially make on-demand services like movies and taxis available in the palm of our hands.

The graveyard is the richest place in the world because that's where everyone dies with their inventions, ideas, engineering concepts, and vertical business processes. Remember, it is easy to follow someone through a minefield. Now is the time to rise and shine, to turn your fear into everything you were created to be by being outcome focused. I dare you to have a die-hard commitment towards your vision.

There is only one way and that's success. There's no plan B because that alone represents an expectation to fail, which is exactly what will happen. Burn the ship and pursue your vision with a burning passion. Make success your best revenge. You will be challenged to quit because that's your inner demon, the dark mindset releasing fear. It's easier to quit than finish what you've started.

I have been poor and that was hard, and I have been rich and that was also hard. Guess which "hard" I chose. Most adversities are self-created. It's you versus *you* in this world. You are your greatest ambassador, and your worst enemy. Once you have manifested your vision and achieved your goal, you will find freedom, and realize how clear everything seems.

Who do you think decides your success? If you stated "Me!" you are correct!

Let's take a quick look at Coca Cola. This company sold only nine servings daily when they launched in Atlanta decades ago. Today, Coca Cola sells over 1.9 billion servings per day. This is an example of an entity that started small and ended colossal. With the right recipe and the right passion driving your vision you can do the same and conquer the world. Elon Musk and Jeff Bezos have put their dent in the universe, as well. Why not put your own dent in mankind's universe by manifesting excellence, by living an extraordinary life full of purpose, by contributing to society and to your personal life?

Let's get into the zone. Let's be genuine: How badly do you want your dreams to become a reality? Be hungry—super hungry—because it is predicted, with very high accuracy, that to attain a goal, what makes the difference is what is done with the gifts of life. Background doesn't matter. Home life or schooling doesn't matter…what does matters is what you DO with your many opportunities. Do you give them away or do you unwrap them carefully?

Remember your mind is like a crowded house—it will sound as if a lot of voices fill your head, so make sure it is filled with positive, motivating, inspirational thoughts to keep focused on the end game.

Your vision takes brain power, and lots of it. The brain is an energy field, and it's been proven through computer simulations that neuron layers travel in electric fields across the brain. The body is made of energy and the sun gives us energy. These are all elementary explanations to demonstrate that we are energy fields, a source of energy to manifest our futures.

In a sense we put a crystal ball in our hand, foretelling what is to come, except this time, it's a written statement and game plan of what the future looks like and when to anticipate the arrival of said manifestation.

It's time to invest in self and build an empire so that you can leave a legacy behind. Whoever controls the thoughts of the mind wins. I have had many consultations where I help entrepreneurs create a one-hundred-year business plan. That alone is a revelation for each person who does this. Why, because during the process of about an hour, the "aha moment," the realization of what that person visualizes is out in front of them. It is like an out of body experience.

Manifesting is like growing a garden, you plant the seed that first develops a root, which is not seen, and then you see the stem pop out and within days and weeks you have the fruit you can enjoy.

It's time to start nurturing that vision to manifest your goal. It will take some time to groom your passion into a reality that you can enjoy—the accomplishment of massive success. Either we are going big, or we're not even trying because, either you're committed to excellence or you're a bystander. Don't try to make it too complicated.

Einstein said it best, "There's genius in simplicity."

Keep it simple. As character develops, you'll grow from child to adult. The stronger your vision manifests the more impact it has. Then it generates the compound effect.

A vision board contains representations of your Big Why. The *How* is your logic—like a scoreboard displaying your numbers. It's going to take everything you've got so forget about trying to figure out how to do this on your own, learn from the best and then, when you've mastered the technique, you can tweak it to suit your needs.

Practice makes perfect. You don't have the evidence of the value from what you can learn from others, who have tried and true results. So, stop discounting yourself and try this process first, and then you can explore more.

Treat this book as a mentorship program because it will be your number one value. You're a winner, so invest in yourself. You can't quit because winners are never quitters. Be relentless in your pursuit for reaching your goals. Manifesting your goals into reality is a science—it's an energy field that is part of your paradigm and your being.

Now you need to harness your manifestation *by meditating on what you want to attract into your life.* That is something you can do early in the morning or when you go to bed at night. There are many online systems for meditating. You can always go to www.WebsiteLink.com for a free version. I used these to achieve all my goals, and if I have said it before, I will say it again; I have accomplished every single goal I have ever set.

Here is the manifestation technique process I practice when I wake up in the morning while still in bed:

Select It, Project It, Collect It.

1. Count down from fifty to one (50 to 1). Count down from whatever number works for you.

2. Get a clear image in your mind of what you desire.

3. Speak out to the universe about what you want—stay positive and be grateful. Ask the Creator of the Universe for answers.

If you can do this three times a day—morning, noon, and before bedtime—you'll begin to see that what you have selected, is projected, and eventually collected.

Visualize your success
then take action.

- Anonymous

Chapter 8
The Flow

THE DAY MY LIFE CHANGED forever. Yes, literally! It was the day I finished a book titled *The Power of Positive Thinking* by Norman Vincent Peale. Here's how this life changing event happened.

I was seventeen years old and a very ambitious and highly motivated businessman, as I used to think of myself at that time. I always carried a business card and seemed to be a nerd at figuring out how to make that next quick dollar. I went to my dad who was an engineer at South African Airlines, a very bright and nerd in his own right...in his field. I asked my pops (another formal name for dad) the big question, "Pops, what is there that I can do to become a better person, do and accomplish great things in life?"

We were sitting at his dark brown round dining room table in his two-bedroom apartment with little furniture—a typical bachelor pad. He looked at me perplexed. I guess he'd never been asked that question before, or he'd never thought of it. He looked at me quite stunned and paused, thinking. He then responded with the best answer that he could think of. He said that he had a friend at his local pub that was a pilot for the airlines and was always buying his wife new BMW's. She was always at the hair salon.

I guessed, my pops being the simple man that he was, thought that he had the answers to life's best kept secrets. Because he was the highest earner in the family (and he complained about how much money his wife spent) his opinion mattered. I love my dad because he's a smart guy in the engineering world, that is. My question wasn't about that…it was about the meaning of life.

Soon thereafter, my pops called me to come over to come and meet his airline pilot that he thought was the best person to answer my question, and he was right. I don't remember the gentleman's name and what I do know is that my dad had just bought me my first car, which was a red mini—the old school British kind. My dad's friend asked (my dad) if he could take it for a drive, just to reminisce.

We met briefly as he explained to me that knowledge was the most powerful gift. This, he surmised, is because one can have all the muscle in the world and be strong. However, if an arm or a leg is lost, that same strong person will starve. If the mind is fed and becomes intellectual, nobody can take that away—that person owns it! I never was one for hard labor. Nor was I a big brute that played rugby or any kind of a rough contact sport, so those words resonated with me.

Dad's friend also told me to read a book titled *The Power of Positive Thinking*. He said that the concepts in that book would help navigate my mind into productive thinking. I said I would get the book straight away. My dad jumped in and said that he was going to get me the book, instead…so, that was taken care of. As I left, I realized I didn't own even one single book. I think I might have had a Bible, but maybe not. I had read the books school gave me and, even then, I didn't care much because I was a total miscreant at school, and never, ever cared about grades or doing homework.

My attitude towards education was probably the worst a person could have. I was not one bit interested in school, and found it consumed way too much of my time. I could have been a different child had I given it my all and, at least, finished school. Because I didn't have a choice, I hated school and thought nothing highly about it. Shortly thereafter, my dad actually surprised me with the book. He'd left it on the dining room table because we rarely crossed paths at home. I picked up the book and read the summary on the back. It explained how positive thoughts and faith can make your life better and foster strength. Gateways of tranquility and the power of the mind were possible!

I don't know what compelled me to read it. I went to my single bed mattress in my room and began reading it on my bed. I honestly don't know what grabbed me the most. There were so many "aha's" written on those pages. I think the fact hit me that if I could connect with other people on the same level of interest or desire, it would make doing business with them easier.

Something in *The Power of Positive Thinking* ignited a fire in my belly. I never felt the same again. I looked at everything differently. Nothing seemed normal or just okay anymore. I looked at life with a sharp eye and analyzed every step. Thought and purpose drove me from then on. The stories in that book almost twenty years ago gave me direction in life. I finished the book in record time and was so impressed that I gave it to my friend to read, never to see it again. Sadly, I think my friend never read the book.

At about this time I began to be overly ambitious, and my endeavors—over the top courageous. I began making more money than any seventeen-year-old could possibly make.

I had traveled from South Africa to the United States buying, trading, and negotiating my way through the global garment industry—of epic proportions. All of this started when I was seventeen—just seventeen. Now, twenty years later I am finding myself proclaiming this same fire in my belly. It ignites my existence—a second chance if you want to call it that. I went from sleeping on my office lobby's sofa to running a half billion-dollar company because I believed I was better than just being average. I wasn't just normal or okey-dokey—I was epic and I knew it.

When you desire in your heart for that vision you have of your life, nothing stops you. You have a goal like that car, a dream home, a love relationship, and of course money. You can attract anything into your life through action and using intention behind the words you speak is a big part of the action needed to bring into creation your desire. I am passionate about improving oneself through expectation.

The more you desire in life the better you become as a person. An affirmation statement vocalizes the desire. By using affirmation, you praise with words, expressing the outcome you expect.

Napoleon Hill was one of the first self-help authors in American history. His book, *Think and Grow Rich* is in the Top 10 best-selling books of all time. He was infatuated with helping people improve their lives. I even asked my eleven-year-old to read the book then took him to a seminar about thinking and growing rich. I don't believe he fully grasped the impact of the thought process designed to get him into this realm. But he was willing and seemed interested. Today he's almost twenty, a successful music producer with endless talent as a DJ and in the music industry.

One of my favorite books is over 700 pages—way too much to comprehend. Rumor has it that Henry Ford told Napoleon Hill to write a watered-down version of said book, and that the new edition was released in 1937. *The Law of Success* is like the Bible of business, which is why I keep a copy on my desk, to remind me of greatness at our fingertips.

I use the law of success to attract the Universe's energy into my life. I started by spending the one-hour commute to the office talking to myself and discussing with myself why I thought it was so important to have the desires of my heart. These became my mantras and developed into affirmations that I recite daily.

Below are a few of these affirmations that I would not only speak into existence on my commute to work but found myself whispering during the whole day—whispering while I went about my day-to-day activities.

- I am wealth.

- I am prosperity.

- I am abundance.

- I am money.

- I am manifestation.

- I am law of attraction.

- I change my subconscious.

- I attract avalanches of prosperity.

- I am positive healing.

- I am positive energy.

- I am trust.

- I am infinite intelligence.

- I am flowing with a Billionaire presence.

- I am attracting abundance.

- I have meaning, purpose, and direction.

- God the creator of the universe is the source of my soul, my life force, the universal truth, and the reason I am alive.

- I receive money every day.

- I receive millions of dollars in my bank.

- I am rich.

- I am powerful.

- I attract money.

- I deserve money.

- I am surrounded with money.

- Money loves me.

- Money flows to me.

- I attract money.

- I have multiple sources of income.
- I am abundant.
- I am highly driven and motivated to succeed.
- I have the ability to make large amounts of money.
- I achieve whatever I set my mind to
- I am focused.
- I attract money easily in every way.
- I am a money master.
- I feel good having money.
- I am prosperous in every way.
- I am successful.
- I am a millionaire.
- I attract all the money I desire.
- I attract people and situations that will help me.
- I choose to be wealthy.
- Money wants me.
- My talent has infinite possibilities.
- My thoughts are positive.
- I am highly ambitious and super motivated to achieve massive success.
- I am completely dedicated to building my wealth.

- I am on the path to reaching massive abundance.

- I have the ability to make lots and lots of money.

- I am already ridiculously rich.

- My state of mind is hyper focused on achieving great amounts of wealth.

- I have unstoppable courage in my ability to succeed.

- Success is my best revenge.

- I have the desire to reach great heights of success.

- Fantastic wealth is headed my way.

- I think positively and attract a one-of-a-kind life for myself.

- Whatever I have set my mind on, I achieve.

- I am rich beyond my wildest dreams.

- I am making lots and lots of money.

- I see millions of dollars in my bank account.

- I am effortlessly attracting millions of dollars.

- I will succeed at the highest level.

- I will become rich and famous because it makes me feel good.

- I am a purposeful driven success making machine.

- I am hyper focused on making money.

- I am becoming the great man God created me to be.

- I am an extraordinary person.

- Making money is easy.

- Happiness, Wealth and health are normal for me.

- I am a leaving a legacy for my children's children.

- I enjoy making millions and millions of dollars.

- I know who I am, I am greatness in the making.

The goal is to make
your heartbeat match
your desired goal.

- Kevin Du Toit

Chapter 9
Focus on the Destination

I WAS ONCE ON A coaching call being held by a very successful mentor whom I admired because he was overly ambitious, made a lot of money, and had his hand in many different types of business. It was an early warm Southern California morning call. He had asked the other entrepreneur if it was ok for me to be in on the call, which was fine with them. I had been on some very serious coaching calls and this one was interesting because it was my *"aha"* moment. I realized that he wasn't so much a coach as he was a relationship counselor. He was helping this entrepreneur navigate managing her staff and sales professionals. I sat in my car thinking to myself, *oh wow! All we are doing is helping people deal with people.*

That's what coaching is all about. Having an accountability partner helps you deal with the day-to-day activities of the office environment, filled with people's issues. Most of the issues stem from emotional responses instead of logical ones, and it's our duty as leaders to redirect that energy into a constructive and productive focus. Remember, the minute you give authority to someone without experience or understanding (how to handle these types of situations), it almost inevitably ends up in chaos.

Everything in life is earned. Sadly, if priceless opportunities haven't been earned, people generally squander those opportunities. This is because the purpose of leadership is to accumulate solutions to draw from in times of need. A transformation took place as my mentor coached the client through the storm, not allowing the weak links to break, and held the team together. It was awe inspiring! Even the most successful people hit stumbling blocks. While these people already know the answer to most problems, it's in times of stress that they seem to lose the plot and need help to rediscover it. This was a super successful coach and a very bright entrepreneur having a very intense discussion, and I was in the grandstands watching the game unfold.

The client actually recognized the problem and how to solve it. It all came down to one thing: Action.

The client had a hard time with the employee because he didn't want to have to reprimand anyone...the results could have been very negative. Either way it didn't matter because the employee did wrong, and he had to suffer the natural consequences of his action. This was not the entrepreneur's problem. I completely understood both sides of the situation. Sadly, it was hard for the entrepreneur to have to discipline the employee and sadly, the employee needed to be corrected to maintain the business' integrity in services and brand recognition.

All that had to be done, at that point, was to take action. Action solves everything. This was my *aha* moment: Action solves everything!

Aside from the realization that we're in the people's dream-making business, all I needed to say was *"Action solves everything!"*

The currency of wealth is time, not money. It's clear most know what it will need to take to reach their goals. One can't be chasing a balloon all the time. It takes a game plan, a mini business plan showing what the goal looks like exactly. In a sense, this is a map to reach a goal, a timeline, and the money needed to make it happen.

Just three elements, a map, timeline, and how much it will cost. There is always a cost to doing business and that is why we need to know what it will take financially to achieve our goals, or what effort it will take to reach sales goals and make that absolutely, ridiculous bonus. How to accomplish the end goal in mind isn't something anyone can just let happen, to "wing it" and see what hits. It must be planned out. A strategy of how you're going to crush it on a monthly, weekly, and daily basis. How many hours will you need? This will be a part of the timeline you'll design to reach your peak performance in achieving your end of game goal.

Do you know exactly what to do in an entire week? If you do, then you are on a fast and furious trajectory to nail your timeline and hit your goal straight on the head. Let's look at a quick exercise to see how much time (out of the one-hundred sixty-eight (168) hours you use up in a one-week period:

168 Hours in a Week
8 hrs. a Night of sleep x7 = 56 hrs.
8 hrs. of work x5 days = 40 hrs.
2 hrs. a day commute x5 = 10 hrs.

1 hr. to get ready for work x5 = 5 hrs.
1 hr. for dinner x7 = 7 hrs.
2 hr. for church x1 = 1 hr.
2 hrs. Grocery shopping = 1 hr.

TOTAL Hours Used 120
AVAILABLE Hours 48

Wake up and give yourself a raise. So far, we've only used up one hundred and twenty (120) hours. So, what are you doing with the other forty-eight (48) hours? I am sure you can find a lot of activities to fill in that time like watching TV, reading the news, surfing the web, and hearing everything posted on social media. I have a saying in my office that if it is not on my calendar, it doesn't exist. I treat my calendar like a time royale. I have everything from the time I wake up at 3:30 a. m., to my studies, prayer and meditation, to my entire work schedule. Then dinner with family, and even an hour of reading at night before I go to bed at 9:00 p. m.

Maximize time to its fullest extent! We've all heard the saying, "You can't buy time," well, we can control our time, as much as possible. Don't allow time to own you or have authority over you. Demand control over every aspect of your day so that you have to mastery of time management. The way you do that is to have your calendar permanently open, preview it as often as possible during the day, and focus on what your day will look like for you successfully.

Call me what you want, but I do this faithfully—I own my destiny and the outcome of my decisions. In order to master myself, I know I need to manage every aspect of my life to get the most out of every moment. I would rather be labeled "obsessive" than "normal" about this topic because "normal" can be too boring.

I want you to be extraordinary and that is going to take some redirection of energy and accountability.

Start with a calendar of events and label it with colors. This helps because when you see a color (for example: green might mean money making time or red might mean a meeting or appointment that can't be missed). For me, orange means follow-up and follow through on projects, financials, and calls. Blue means lunch (I, actually, do take lunch, which is never wasted. I am either reading a book, watching a YouTube video, or catching up on my social media content).

There are lots of ways to make money but the one thing that can't be bought back is time. There are no scratch-and-get-rich-quick scheme or overnight success schemes out there, they're all nonsense. A confession: I used to spend three hours a day on average on social media. Once, I tracked my time spent on reading bitesize content and not focusing on myself. Shocking! So, I changed my process to previewing social media as I walk from my car to the office and in the elevator. Once I enter the office, I stop the social media activity.

I came up with the idea that, as a reward, on every hour of my workday, I give myself the last ten minutes to scroll through social media. I need this "fix" to keep me going. I know it's not healthy, and that is my downfall. I love the social media button that is also a huge part of my business, so the reason is for marketing. But the excuse I give myself is to get a glimpse of what my family is up to and see what's trending all over the world.

Taking control of my time has led to more productivity, something I still work on daily. This is because life is hectic, and that I find myself constantly updating my schedule because circumstances change—nothing is perfect, and things just come up. On occasion, I must drop whatever it is I am doing and redirect my focus on that particular task. That's called being flexible. I have taught myself to be ok with change, I can never control how events roll out. What I can control is the outcome, so I become flexible to the point that I don't allow issues to steal my joy.

I planted my flag and developed a work ethic to support myself and my goals, because nothing happens in life without the necessary effort.

The struggle is real. But the more you resist an issue, the more it affects you internally. So, take ownership and focus on polishing skills and ability. How can anyone expect to accomplish anything in life without a chartered course of action, a game plan, or business plan. Before a cruise ship leaves port, it knows exactly where it's going, how to get there, and precisely how long it will take to arrive. Its GPS navigates automatically as the captain makes sure the ship maintains course. When a decision is made to change course, the cruise ship turns slowly. Think of this analogy: You are the cruise ship, and your brain is the captain. What course are you going to take? Will you choose a course that reaches your desired destination? The answer is likely, "Of course!" That's why we're on this journey of self-mastery.

So, why do so many people vainly brag about how amazing they're doing, and yet in reality, they have no idea about what "being amazing" means. I'm not talking about doing great at a day job that requires you to log in at 9:00 a. m. and log out at 5:00 p. m. That person gives away his dreams to his employer. The boss is essentially living the employee's dreams because that employee allowed the boss to inherit it. The day you choose to be uncommon among the uncommon, you begin to find purpose. Then, you can develop a vision of staying hyper-focused on your goals, your wants, and needs. Those come first, everything else is secondary.

Again, it's like chasing a balloon. Create an action plan. Don't allow the winds of whatever the days brings to blow you in any direction. Stop using a magnifying glass and start to thoroughly enjoy life.

It's time to dream, and dream big, because if those on the outside don't scoff at your vision, then it's not big enough. You're in the right place, at the right time. Yes, your journey will sometimes be lonely. There's a reason they say, "It's lonely at the top." If so, you're in the right place, at the right time. You choose to do what you want to do, and I commend you for stepping out of a normal routine.

The achievement of goals is your new *How*, and you can't think like a spectator, sitting in the grandstands of life watching A players and B players in action. You have to participate and accomplish. It might seem tough and rather hard to create a vision board, and then to create a game plan from that of how you want to accomplish your vision. But remember, adversity toughens you up and gives you a sense of purpose and clarity in your destiny.

A technique, a method of conducting business is very valuable. Take a look at Uber, Airbnb, Amazon, and even McDonalds. Creating your own game plan is simple and very valuable. For instance, if you want to write a book it will take you approximately forty hours, depending on the content and its length. So, schedule one or two hours a day. Normally, I will write first thing in the morning when there are no distractions, it's peaceful, the sun is rising, and God speaks…and everyone in my household is sleeping.

My time for writing is from 4:30 AM to 6:30 a. m. Then I stop and begin to get ready for my day. That's also the time my family wakes up. The same goes for exercise, meditation, prayer, reading, business planning, and writing out affirmations. By the way, the biggest part of the day is when you write your affirmations.

Consider writing your own personal affirmations—your life's "creed"—a formal statement of guidelines and beliefs you would repeat daily and meditate upon. Connect with me for guidance on how to do this. I'll gladly share my personal advice and "tips" for writing affirmations with you because it's important—a very powerful mind over matter formula.

Schedule in your calendar daily events and objectives. That way, if you miss a day, you can always start from where you left off. Don't try to do a catch-up day, it will overwhelm you and you'll never get anything accomplished. Just begin where you ended off. The best time is always *now*. Don't procrastinate and push it off.

Plan a schedule. The number one thing people fail to do is follow up with their scheduled activities and objectives. Most times, people simply lose focus. The number two failure is a lack of follow through. Nothing is completed as a result. Follow-up and follow-through are the key ingredients in any successful activity. You can make things happen in your life with little effort by just following up on what needs to be completed, and then following through to accomplish it.

The following story is one of my favorites where behavior kicks into play. This is the story of the bamboo farmer.

There was a Chinese farmer who planted bamboo seeds in his field. Every day, he went outside and watered, and cared for his newly planted bamboo farm. The locals started to mock him because there was still nothing after the first year. Then, on the second year, and again, the third and fourth year—NOTHING. Even so, the Chinese bamboo farmer wasn't deterred by the limited faith of his neighbors. He knew they didn't see what he envisioned. Suddenly, in the fifth year, green sprouts emerged from the barren ground. Within six weeks the bamboo had grown, and grown, and grown...to reach more than ninety feet high.

Your journey is exactly the same as the process of the Chinese bamboo tree: *A lot* of nurturing must take place. Your field of dreams requires a lot of seed planting and watering. By showering your life with positive words—even affirmations—so that the energy can bring the greatness out of you. No one ever sees the immediate results of goals set until time has passed. Then, in the future, the blessing comes. Refuse to give up. Keep up your courage and you'll receive victories repeatedly from persistence.

Be selfish! Be very selfish. It's totally okay.

Sort yourself out first before you try to save others. Remember, *you* are the person who needs saving. That's why it is crucial in the development process, you build up the desire to reach your destination and finally receive the award of achieving your goal.

I believe we're all on a hero's or heroine's journey in life. We choose which direction we want to take by the decisions we make, giving us a cause-and-effect outcome. I spent most of my years in Hollywood: sixteen and one-half years, to be precise, working at DreamWorks SKG and Amblin Entertainment that was Steven Spielberg's campus on the Universal Studios Lot.

I worked on movies ranging from *Saving Private Ryan*, *Gladiator* (my favorite experience), and even the *E. T.* re-release that was a dream come true. *E. T.* was a childhood memory and I worked on the new re-release! What a privilege! This is a prime example of achieving goals. Because I went to Hollywood to work for Steven Spielberg, within two years, I was right there amongst the Hollywood elite. It was pretty mind-blowing. Alas, that's a whole other book. In those years of living in Los Angeles and working as a Production Assistant on movie sets to working with the royalty of Hollywood…well, that is a major movie within itself.

The point I am trying to make is that it was a dream, a goal, a vision. I held onto that vision and within two years, I not only worked for Steven Spielberg but was fortunate enough to mingle with the most incredible human beings in the world, and to work hand-in-hand with them all. This is where all my storytelling comes from, and my screenplays. One of them *Tau Ya Soweto* won the Humane Society Award (it was later taken away because of botched up judging credits—a pretty interesting sequence of events). I also won the Bear Award for Best Screenplay for "Cape Flats" at the Berlin Film Festival.

Almost two decades in Hollywood, reading hundreds of scripts, automatically embedded into my subconscious mind the formula for writing. That's how I believe my screenplays got where they did. There is a magic to storytelling, and Steven Spielberg tells them the best. I also read and studied at the New York Film Academy on screenplay writing. I believe that's what allowed me to understand the story, about a mythological hero's adventures that takes place from our world into the supernatural realm. There, the hero discovers fabulous forces and becomes the victor! He returns from his mysterious journey with a magical power which he awards to his people. It is the most popular theme or template that showcases a hero, who goes on an epic adventure, wins some battles, and then returns home, transformed.

All things considered, we all should be in the same place by now—you, who are thoroughly enjoying this book as you go on to self-mastery and discovery of the untapped potential that lies within and is just now waking up. Let's call it "The Great Awakening." Exciting!

There will be lots of ups and downs along your journey as you climb. A zigzag of paths will challenge you as you strive to reach the top of your peak. Highly successful people rarely aim for the top of their business mountain in a straight line, they know the passage has many stumbling blocks and obstacles to overcome—that's part of the process.

Keep your mind hyper-focused on your goal and let your body do all the action. It's leveraged in a worldly kind of way: You're using brain power to guide your physical being in the direction it needs to go.

Every now and then, the need occurs to redirect or re-evaluate circumstances, and possibly tweak the system or technique to make it a better one. That's okay because these are lessons accumulated along the way to greatness. To accomplish anything great, one needs to become great.

As you attain the ability and power to harness the body and mind towards your desired goal, you will go into a shift, a good shift, that sets you free the closer you get to the goal.

Whenever I set a goal, I surround myself with an image of the item, a dollar sign, or the destination I envision and place it on my vision board, cell phone, and computer screensavers. This is so that I always have a constant reminder of my purpose and the goal I am planning to attain. These images are never out of sight. At every turn, I am reminded. Every time I use my cell phone, log onto my computer, or scroll across my vision board I am reminded. I even attach pictures into my journals. Journals are key "tools" kept by successful people. In journals, successful ideas are written. My many journals contain one-liners I've heard in the past (many are included in this book), stories I want to recollect, and reminders of concepts I don't want to forget. Like yours, my mind has tens of thousands of thoughts in a day.

Experts estimate that the mind thinks between 60,000 – 80,000 thoughts daily (Sasson, 2022). Men use about seven thousand (7,000) words a day while women use three times more than men.

Silence is a powerful weapon, which is why you need to fuel your subconscious mind with positive content for an abundant productive and radiant life. Be cautious of your thoughts. Allow only positivity into your mind's thoughts. Our consciousness is fed by our subconscious, making us unique in a sense that fear, doubt, procrastination, and negativity make up our limiting beliefs. That negativity sabotages performance.

Now that you are feeding your mind with positive, productive content, and mediating on future goals, use caution in your associations. Be aware of the positive or negative influence of those around you. Without a doubt, if you show me your friends, I'll show you where success dwells. You become who you surround yourself by. Mostly, it's loved ones, friends, and your coworkers. Those who live with negative outlooks are the most poisonous and will infect. Your capability of reaching God-given talents will be thwarted unless you are selective with whom you choose to spend your time around. Choose those who emulate the same integrity and inner strength you seek.

By now, you have begun to form a behavior most commonly labeled "a habit." Several different versions of what creates a habit are circulating "out there." Here are two: twenty-one days or sixty-sixty days are required to set a habit. Either way, once the process is established, through frequent repetition, the behavior becomes a habit. Habits are provoked by either observing someone else or through creating a routine. These habits will help us reach our goals. In your DNA there is a genetic history that also drives who you become. You inherit behaviors from your parents, teachers, and those closest to you. Pay attention to those and make conscious decisions accordingly. The cycles of behavior can be broken with conscientious attention to them.

By applying all that you've read and understood along your personal journey, you're partaking in becoming your own advocate to reach your goals. An action you repeat will become habitual. Eventually, those actions (or habits) seem a normal part of who you are and how you operate in life. This is the new cycle you've created that can be drawn upon to reach goals.

Remember: Action solves everything.

Consistently doing the same thing over and over again, over a period of time compounds upon itself into abundant energy. The results aren't immediate, they are compounding.

Most likely, you will notice this energy from habit within ninety days.

Creating Your Manifestation:

1. Time block, plan in your calendar to meditate.

2. Compliment and acknowledge yourself when reaching landmarks.

3. Speak out your affirmations into existence.

A vibration is a state of being,
the energy of a person, and
the thought of an ideal.

- Kevin Du Toit

HERE'S A SECRET

Within this chapter are the tools to recognize and produce an avalanche of abundance. This happens when your thoughts, through organized chaos, create the energy to manifest success. It's like a river that naturally flows into an ocean of abundance. Think about abundance and you will grow an avalanche of prosperity.

Think it and you will *Be* it.

A book that sits-alone on my office describes our bodies as temples. Now and then, our lives allow us to peer into our souls through our sacred temples.

The divine ideal of oneself is self-mastery:

i·de·al

satisfying one's conception of what
is perfect; most suitable.

I often refer to this particular book that looks like a glorified Bible with its thick, black, covered case and thin pages with the fore-edges etched in gold. I want to cover concepts I've developed from working the concepts in this book. People I've helped to integrate the same concepts have been impacted. This is what I want for you, too, dear reader.

Dale Carnegie, famous for his self-improvement books and hundreds of interviews with millionaires across America, had many one-on-one meetings with industrial giants like Thomas Edison, Henry Ford, John D. Rockefeller, J. P. Morgan and Henry Ford to name a few.

The men he associated with were extraordinary human beings. These men understood the collective laws that are considered "doorways" to the organized foundations of our universe, our collective energy. Much like the Biblical tree of life, it's an understanding of the knowledge of good and evil. Once you take part in the fruit of the tree of life you eat and live forever. Once you feed your brain with knowledge and understanding, a similar transformation occurs: you become unstoppable.

Your desire for superior knowledge overwhelms your senses because you want more. In truth, you'll find that you can't believe you didn't know what you didn't know, and your brain will be hungry for more. You'll never be the same once you've stretched your imagination and expanded your thoughts—it can't go back to its original size. Once you have defined your purpose, you become more effective in your day-to-day activities. You will automatically find time to set priorities, block out time on your calendar, and execute tasks. Many people waste their day by staying busy at keeping themselves busy—they're doing "busy stuff" but ultimately accomplish little to nothing at all. This is called non-productive work.

Proper planning is just like meal preparation. The tools include a recipe, the ingredients, items with which to cook, manipulation of all the above into chemical reactions that are delectable, and finally, it's time to imbibe in the creation. Life is exactly the same; instead of living aimlessly through life, take charge and create a recipe for a healthier, happier, and wealthier life.

Be hyper focused on making your heart and mind one. Feel the energy from your toes to the hairs on your head. Now, put that same feeling of energy out into the universe, and begin a recipe for success by writing down, using an organizer to plan your entire day, and move forward with those plans. From the time you wake up, you will have a well-conceived vision of what your day will look like at the get-go. Of course, you can always tweak your events as the day goes on, when needed, but the most important thing is that you at least have it mapped out, a game plan, a plan of attack. When you look back, you'll see from all the preparing and planning that the outcome was a result of the course you took, and you reached your destiny.

Self-mastery is an accumulation of many mindset traits.

THE SHIFT happens when GOD - ENERGY – YOU work "THE WHY POWER"

To accomplish anything great, you must become great. Let us cover three traits to develop in order to properly access and execute dreams:

- Self-confidence—an understanding of self-worth.

- Initiative—to become a leader.

- Imagination—to take action.

Take a look at the SEO of what self-confidence and self-worth means.

self-con·fi·dence

A feeling of trust in one's abilities,
qualities, and judgment.

self-worth

A sense of one's own value as a human being.

Self-mastery is the overcoming of the basics and fears. It is overcoming self-doubt and a belief that one is worthy only of poverty. This is a falsehood we feed to ourselves. With enough feeding, we begin to believe this nonsense as truth. It isn't! This type of false belief is merely a lack of wholesome mentality and impending spiritual death. The ego tells one thing, while self-confidence states something entirely different. Self-confidence, the belief and *knowing* of who we are in God's eyes is based upon definite truth, usable knowledge.

Self-worth is having a deep understanding of your value, your self-esteem. It's knowing that if someone were to offer you a job, you'd know your worth and how much that would cost the employer. Most people are not aware of their inherent worth. A good way to figure that out is to observe someone you admire, or respect. What is their inherent value? Can you tell just by looking at them?

Let's use a basic estimate. For example, a Life Coach's annually earnings is approximately $70,000 (seventy thousand dollars). Take $70,000 and divide that by 12 months, giving you $5,833 per month. Now divide $5,833 by 4 weeks in a month, giving you $1,458 per week. Divide $1,458 by 10 hours of work per week, and the base hourly rate is $36 (I rounded off the numbers to keep the math simple). Now, a Life Coach knows that his basic hourly rate (what someone will pay for his services) is $36 an hour to coach them.

Is that figure too low for you? You bet it is!

So, double that number, triple it, even 10x's the number, because you will get paid what your self-confidence is telling you you're worth.

Knowing what you are worth at an hourly rate will help you determine what you need to do in order to attain that income goal. There are many ways to figure out how to reach your income goals, be it more education, another certification, or moving to a location with less taxes and/or better economic growth in the marketplace.

Take initiative and become a Leader.

Everyone has leadership qualities within. Those who make a conscious decision to take charge of their life, their well-being, their destiny; become leaders in their own right. One of the first traits of becoming a leader is to take accountability for your actions. Never have someone else do an important task or goal for you, take initiative and do it yourself.

Action leads to purpose.

Action solves everything. Taking action will reveal all kinds of challenges most have never anticipated. This is a good sign! It shows growth and the ability to stretch the mind's creativity (imagination) to find solutions. This is where ideas are hatched, where people figure out solutions and make plans to solve problems. The mind is so powerful! It's your own super-computer. When you initiate an action, all kinds of energy spark to illuminate how to become a much better leader, instead of becoming a follower. You are grooming yourself for excellence without even knowing it. You are developing skills by stretching your imagination beyond its normal capacity.

In South Africa we have a saying, "A boer (farmer) makes a plan." Meaning, with limited resources, out in the deep bushveld of Africa, one needs to make plans—this with limited resources—in order to survive.

The same is in our daily lives. Money solves a lot of problems however we don't all have endless amounts of money available. Action leads to purpose. So, use your God given gift, your brain, to come up with complex solutions and ways to implement those solutions.

Imagination creates opportunity.

Imagination is everything, and, as you know, it is more powerful than knowledge. Without it, mass media just entertains with mindless content. To enhance yourself, your mind needs to be set free so that all your hopes and desires in life become a reality. We wouldn't have the electric car, space travel, or sustainable living available today if someone hadn't used their imagination. Whenever anyone thinks he's nailed a new idea, you'll see that same person act with due diligence to see if his idea is a new innovative concept. If not, that same forward-thinker will find a way to creatively do things differently. Sometimes we are prompted with divine ideas and gifts that we sometimes ignore. Those promptings may be the next billion-dollar idea! Taking any kind of action on a newly conceived idea will help to build a foundation upon which to improve. Your mind is a goldmine of precious value proposition, it provides the contribution needed to build a legacy.

Enthusiasm sells your story.

I once was given the opportunity to pitch a movie script to the president of DreamWorks SKG. He was a young dynamic and super successful executive who had green-lit many of the box office hits that movie-goers know of today. My pitch lasted less than two minutes as he stared at me with a blank face. I knew I had lost him. He told me to place my pitch on his desk and he would review it later, and then he asked me to move in closer. I shook with fear!

He said, "You're missing one key ingredient to your story!" I was pleased he hadn't chased me out of his office, so, I listened intently. "Enthusiasm," he continued. "You have a good story. However, your pitch isn't exciting. It didn't move me. I couldn't connect."

I walked out of that once-in-a-lifetime opportunity remembering one thing: Enthusiasm is most important. That was the one key take-away that resonates with me to this day, almost twenty years later. Sell your idea by telling a story, *with enthusiasm.*

Self-control is self-mastery.

This should be every single human's goal—the end game in life: Be a life-learner that allows abilities to constantly evolve. Take on new hobbies, or a course to update or add more credentials to your skill sets. Make yourself an asset to your job and to your family. You are the most valuable asset you know—pumping your mind, body, and soul with positive and productive content will make you even more unique. You will set yourself apart from the crowd because you have elevated yourself.

Conclusion
The Magical Equation

BE (purpose)   DO (Action)   HAVE (Reward)

LET ME SUM THIS UP for you: BE is discovering your purpose, DO is taking massive action, and HAVE is the realization of all the rewards you earned along the way.

I hope you enjoyed this journey through the path to success. These concepts had an impact on me. The day I finished writing this book, I was filled with a rejuvenated feeling of want—to create more, do more, and even come up ideas for my next book.

We began this journey together, to discover self-mastery and self-worth, to create a life by design. Each of us is on our own journey to make our dreams a reality!

Thank you, thank you, and thank you for sharing this journey with me. May you discover all of your hopes, desires and dreams.

The journey continues…

Resources

Peale, D. N. V. (1990). *The power of positive thinking.*
Cedar Books.

Silva, A. (2022) *The Alan Silva Method.*

> https://silvamethod.com/?gclid=CjwK-
> CAjw3K2XBhAzEiwAmmgrAjDB3yky
> CGIHPULVdsV4o4oQw10iSv_W8jtyD57USrlFnHw3-
> MEv1RoC_LIQAvD_BwE

Byrne, R. (2021) *The secret documentary—DVD.*

> https://www.thesecret.tv/products/the-secret-film-dvd/

Wattles, W., (2010). *Wallace D. Wattles.* Simon & Schuster.

> https://www.simonandschuster.com/books/The-
> New-Science-of-Getting-Rich/Wallace-D-Wattles/
> Library-of-Hidden-Knowledge/9781582707112

Cleveland Clinic (2022, May 17). *Body systems and organs.*

> https://my.clevelandclinic.org/health/body/21824-kid-
> ney#:~:text=Your%20kidneys%20filter%20about%20
> 200,body%20as%20urine%20(pee).

Sasson, R. (accessed 2022). How many thoughts does your mind think in one hour? *Success*

Consciousness. https://www.success-consciousness.com/blog/inner-peace/ how-many-thoughts-does-your-mind-think-in-one-hour/

BE - CREATION

DO - TRANSFORMATION

HAVE - COMPLETION

www.ingramcontent.com/pod-product-compliance
Lightning Source LLC
Chambersburg PA
CBHW071017120626
46546CB00003B/1135